How to Use
the
Major Indexes
to
U.S. Government
Publications

John M. Ross

American Library Association

Chicago and London 1989

Text designed by Herb Slobin
Cover designed by Harriett Banner
Type prepared by ALA Books, using a BestInfo Wave 4 prepress system,
   output to Linotronic L–500 by Glenbard Graphics, Inc.
Printed on 50–pound Cougar Opaque, a pH–neutral paper,
   by Imperial Printing Company

The paper used in this publication meets the minimum requirements of
American National Standard for Information Sciences—Permanence of
Paper for Printed Library Materials, ANSI Z39.48-1984.

Library of Congress Cataloging-in-Publication Data

Ross, John M. (John Murray)
   How to use the major indexes to U.S. government publications.
   1. Government publications—United States—Indexes—Handbooks,
manuals, etc. I. Title.
Z1223.Z7R67   1989 [J83]   016.73′053   88-35127
ISBN 0-8389-0509-9 (alk. paper)

Printed in the United States of America

Contents

Introduction

U.S. government publications sources are not really difficult to use. Because they are so different from other reference indexes, most users have trouble mastering them without some assistance. Unfortunately, many users are discouraged after a first attempt and never really work with them at all. U.S. documents should not be overlooked, especially by students and researchers working in the social sciences. People in the sciences should also be familiar with the sources, depending on the nature of their research. Today documents are available through excellent sources that catalog, index, abstract, and analyze them.

This text will show you in a clear, step-by-step process how to use each of the six most important sources for locating U.S. documents. First, the organization of each source is explained. Then examples show how to search for a specific document in each of the sources. You are asked to search for a document similar to the one in the example just covered. Upon finishing each question, turn back to the text and continue until you have answered all the questions. To make sure that you have used the references correctly, check your answers against those at the end of the text.

This text covers only subject indexes, the approach most users take. Once you have mastered this approach, you should have no trouble working with the others.

Not everyone will want to go through the entire text. If you want to use just one or two of the sources, then read only those sections of the text that apply to them.

The function of these sources is explained briefly, but there is no attempt to give a full description of their origin, history, and purpose. The object here is simply to show how to use these reference sources:

American Statistics Index: A Comprehensive Guide and Index to the Statistical Publications of the U.S. Government. Washington, D.C.: Congressional Information Service. Annual, with monthly supplements.

Congressional Information Service. *CIS/Annual.* Washington, D.C.: Congressional Information Service. 3 vols. 1, *Abstracts of Congressional Publications and Legislative Histories.* 2, *Index to Congressional Publications and Public Laws.* 3, *Legislative Histories of U.S. Public Laws.* Vols. 1-2, annual, with monthly supplements; vol. 3, annual.

Index to U.S. Government Periodicals. Chicago: Infordata International. Annual, with quarterly supplements.

U.S. Congress. *Congressional Record: Proceedings and Debates of the Congress.* Washington, D.C.: Government Printing Office. Daily, with biweekly index.

U.S. Superintendent of Documents. *Monthly Catalog of United States Government Publications.* Washington, D.C.: Government Printing Office. Monthly, with semi-annual and annual cumulative indexes.

Monthly Catalog

The oldest and most comprehensive source for locating U.S. documents is the *Monthly Catalog*. Published monthly by the Government Printing Office, it was first issued in 1895 and has continued without interruption to the present. Before 1974 the access to the *Monthly Catalog* was mainly through a subject index. Between 1974 and 1980 seven new indexes were added: Author, Title, Series/Report, Contract Number, Stock Number, Title Keyword, and Classification. All the indexes are issued monthly and are included at the back of each issue of the *Monthly Catalog*. They are cumulated semiannually and annually in separate volumes.

The index most frequently used for researching federal documents is the Subject Index. The examples and exercises given here will be confined to this index. Once you have mastered it, you should have no trouble working with the others.

Using the *Monthly Catalog* is a two-step process. To do a subject search, first, look up the subject in the Subject Index. Having located a relevant entry, look up the number for that entry in the *Monthly Catalog*.

Subject Search Example

Drug abuse is one of the major problems facing the United States today. Let us suppose your topic is on drug abuse prevention. Use the 1986 Subject Index to find what report was released on drug abuse prevention. To find this report, you look up the subject in the index. Figure 1 is part of a page in the index. Titles are listed alphabetically under each subject. After each title is an entry number. The entry

number for the report on drug abuse prevention is 86-498. You now look up the entry number (86-498) for that report in the *Catalog*. The reports are listed in numerical order, starting with 86-1 in the January issue. The numbers contained in each issue are indicated on the spine.

Figure 2 is part of a page from the *Monthly Catalog* citing the entry for that report. To locate this document on the shelf, you need the documents classification number that is always cited above the entry in the center. This is the Superintendent of Documents classification number, commonly referred to as the SuDocs number. You will need this number to locate most U.S. documents on the shelf.

Starting in 1987, the *Monthly Catalog* includes the document classification numbers (SuDocs numbers) in the Subject, Author, and Title indexes. (The other indexes, Series/Report, Title Keyword, etc., continue to give only the entry numbers.) Therefore, in subject searching the *Monthly Catalog* from 1987 and on, there is no need to look up the entry number in the Catalog to find the documents classification number. Compare the examples in figure 3. The Subject Index for 1986 gives only the entry number, whereas the one for 1987 gives both the entry number and the documents classification number.

Subject Search Exercise

Using the 1986 Subject Index of the *Monthly Catalog*, find the title and documents classification number of a report covering drug abuse in Canada.

(For answers to all the exercises, see end of text.)

Dropouts U.S.   **Subject Index**

3042) (including cost estimate of the Congressional Budget Office)., 86-19927

subject

Oversight hearing on successful education programs relating to illiteracy, bilingual education, and dropout prevention : hearing before the Subcommittee on Elementary, Secondary, and Vocational Education of the Committee on Education and Labor, House of Representatives, Ninety-ninth Congress, first session, hearing held in Los Angeles, CA, November 25, 1985., 86-15049

Drops.
Droplet sizes, dynamics, and deposition in vertical annular flow /, 86-16327

Steam generator tube rupture iodine transport mechanisms : Task 1, Experimental studies /, 86-16318

Drug abuse.
Drugs of abuse., 86-1422

Genetic and biological markers in drug abuse and alcoholism /, 86-16959

Patterns and trends in drug abuse : a national and international perspective., 86-8309

Phencyclidine : an update /, 86-11446

Drug abuse — Alaska.
Scope and impact of narcotic trafficking in Alaska : hearing before the Subcommittee on Children, Family, Drugs, and Alcoholism of the Committee on Labor and Human Resources, United States Senate, Ninety-ninth Congress, first session ... August 30, 1985., 86-10783

Drug abuse — Canada.
The Illicit drug situation in the United States and Canada., 86-1421

Drug abuse — Congresses.
Problems of drug dependence., 86-14227

Drug abuse — Illinois — Chicago.
Drug abuse and drug trafficking in Chicago : hearings before the Select Committee on Narcotics Abuse and Control, House of Representatives, Ninety-ninth Congress, first session, May 31-June 1, 1985., 86-9279

Drug abuse — Latin America.
Developments in Latin American narcotics control, November 1985 : hearing before the Committee on Foreign Affairs, House of Representatives, Ninety-ninth Congress, first session, November 12, 1985., 86-10738

Drug abuse — New England.
Drug abuse and drug trafficking in New England : a report of the Select Committee on Narcotics Abuse and Control, Ninety-ninth Congress, second session., 86-20136

Drug abuse — Northeastern States.
Drug abuse and drug trafficking in the Northeast region : hearings before the Select Committee on Narcotics Abuse and Control, House of Representatives, Ninety-ninth Congress, first session, September 20-21, 1985., 86-18935

Drug abuse — Prevention — United States.
title Etiology of drug abuse : implications for prevention /, 86-498 *entry no.*

Drug abuse — Research grants — United States — Statistics — Periodicals.
Alcohol, drug abuse, mental health, research grant awards /, 86-18247

Drug abuse — South Dakota.
Alcohol and drug abuse in South Dakota : hearings before a subcommittee of the Committee on Appropriations, United States Senate, Ninety-ninth Congress, first session : special hearings, Department of the Treasury., 86-10667

Drug abuse — Study and teaching — United States — Bibliography — Catalogs.
Drug education., 86-354

Drug abuse — Study and teaching (Higher) — United States.
Alcohol and drug abuse curriculum guide for pediatrics faculty /, 86-505

Drug abuse — Treatment.
Guide to the addiction severity index : background, administration, and field testing results /, 86-4344

Drug abuse — Treatment — Congresses.
Problems of drug dependence., 86-14227

Drug abuse — Treatment — United States.
Treatment process in methadone, residential, and outpatient drug free programs /, 86-502

Drug abuse — Treatment — United States — Periodicals.
NIDA notes /, 86-11448

State resources and services for alcohol and drug abuse problems /, 86-11450, 86-19329

Treatment research notes /, 86-11447

Drug abuse — Treatment — United States — States — Finance — Periodicals.
State resources and services for alcohol and drug abuse problems /, 86-19329

Drug abuse — Treatment — United States — Statistics — Periodicals.
CODAP quarterly reports, 86-3139

Data from the client oriented data acquisition process, 86-3139

National Institute on Drug Abuse statistical series. Series D, Quarterly report, provisional data. Data from the client oriented data acquisition process., 86-3139

Quarterly report, provisional data. Data from the client oriented data acquisition process, 86-3139

Drug abuse — United States.
Alcohol, drug abuse, and mental health amendments of 1986 : report (to accompany H.R. 5259) (including cost estimate of the Congressional Budget Office)., 86-19970

The clandestine manufacture of illicit drugs : hearings before a subcommittee of the Committee on Government Operations, House of Representatives, Ninety-ninth Congress, first session, September 24, and December 5, 1985., 86-13634

Cocaine abuse and the federal response : hearing before the Select Committee on Narcotics Abuse and Control, House of Representatives, Ninety-ninth Congress, first session, Tuesday, July 16, 1985., 86-17822

Coordinating and expanding services for the prevention, identification and treatment of alcohol and drug abuse among Indian youth, and for other purposes : report (to accompany S. 1298)., 86-9021

Drug abuse in the military : hearing before the Subcommittee on Children, Family, Drugs, and Alcoholism of the Committee on Labor and Human Resources, United States Senate, Ninety-ninth Congress, first session, on reviewing the problem of drug abuse in the military, June 27, 1985., 86-2038

Drug use before and during drug abuse treatment : 1979-1981 TOPS admission cohorts /, 86-500

Drugs and dropouts : a report of the Select Committee on Narcotics Abuse and Control, Ninety-ninth Congress, second session., 86-13681

Drugs of abuse : a supervisor's guide /, 86-6045

The Illicit drug situation in the United States and Canada., 86-1421

Neuroscience methods in drug abuse research /, 86-4342

Patterns and trends in drug abuse : a national and international perspective., - 86-8309

Women and drugs : a new era for research /, 86-15532

Drug abuse — United States — Periodicals.
ADAMHA news /, 86-3134

Drug abuse — United States — Prevention.
Designer drugs, 1985 : hearing before the Subcommittee on Children, Family, Drugs, and Alcoholism of the Committee on Labor and Human Resources, United States Senate, Ninety-ninth

Do not order from index; see indicated entry

Figure 1. Sample page from the Subject Index to the *Monthly Catalog.*

NATIONAL INSTITUTE OF MENTAL HEALTH
Health and Human Services Dept.
Rockville, MD 20857

86-494

HE 20.8102:Ad 9/2

Ageton, Suzanne S.

Facts about sexual assault from the NCPCR National Center for the Prevention and Control of Rape : a research report for adults who work with teenagers / by Suzanne S. Ageton. — Rockville, Md. : U.S. Dept. of Health and Human Services, Public Health Service, Alcohol, Drug Abuse, and Mental Health Administration, National Institute of Mental Health, [1985]

ii, 17 p. ; 23 cm. — (DHHS publication ; no. (ADM) 85-1398) Bibliography: p. 16-17. "Grant number MH 31751"—T.p. verso. ●Item 507-B-5

1. Youth — United States — Sexual behavior. 2. Sex crimes — United States. 3. Rape victims — United States. 4. Rapists — United States. I. National Center for the Prevention and Control of Rape (U.S.) II. Title. III. Series. OCLC 12678615

86-495

HE 20.8102:Se 6/2

Rieman, Dwight W.

Notable solutions to problems in mental health services delivery / Dwight W. Rieman, Richard B. Cravens, Beth A. Stroul. — Rockville, Md. : U.S. Dept. of Health and Human Services, Public Health Service, Alcohol, Drug Abuse, and Mental Health Administration, National Institute of Mental Health, 1985.

vi, 99 p. ; 28 cm. — (DHHS publication ; no. (ADM) 85-1403) Includes indexes. ●Item 507-B-5

1. Community mental health services — United States. 2. Mental health services — United States. I. Cravens, Richard B. II. Stroul, Beth A. III. National Institute of Mental Health (U.S.) IV. Title. V. Series. OCLC 12738375

86-496

HE 20.8102:T 22

Ageton, Suzanne S.

Facts about sexual assault from the NCPCR National Center for the Prevention and Control of Rape : a research report for teenagers / by Suzanne S. Ageton. — Rockville, Md. : U.S. Dept. of Health and Human Services, Public Health Service, Alcohol, Drug Abuse, and Mental Health Administratrion, National Institute of Mental Health, 1985.

15 p. ; 23 cm. — (DHHS publication ; no. (ADM) 85-1397) Shipping list no.: 85-844-P. Bibliography: p. 14-15. "Grant number MH 31751"—T.p. verso. ●Item 507-B-5

1. Youth — United States — Sexual behavior. 2. Sex crimes — United States. 3. Rape victims — United States. 4. Rapists — United States. I. National Center for the Prevention and Control of Rape (U.S.) II. Title. III. Series. OCLC 12660226

1. Mental illness — Prevention — Bibliography. I. Trickett, Edison J. II. Corse, Sara J. III. National Institute of Mental Health (U.S.) IV. Title. V. Series. VI. Series: Primary prevention publication series. [DNLM 1. Mental Health — bibliography 2. Mental Health Services — bibliography 3. Primary Prevention — bibliography] OCLC 12595366

NATIONAL INSTITUTE ON DRUG ABUSE
Health and Human Services Dept.
Rockville, MD 20857

entry no.

86-498

documents class no.

HE 20.8216:56

entry

Etiology of drug abuse : implications for prevention / editors Coryl LaRue Jones, Robert J. Battjes. — Rockville, Md. : Dept. of Health and Human Services, Public Health Service, Alcohol, Drug Abuse, and Mental Health Administration, National Institute on Drug Abuse ; Washington, D.C. : For sale by the Supt. of Docs., U.S. G.P.O., 1985.

viii, 283 p. : ill. ; 24 cm. — (NIDA research monograph ; 56. A RAUS review report) (DHHS publication ; no. (ADM) 85-1335) "This monograph is based upon papers and discussion from a Research Analysis and Utilization Survey (RAUS) review which took place on April 24 and 25, 1984 at Rockville, Maryland. The meeting was sponsored by the Office of Science, National Institute on Drug Abuse"—P. iv. Includes bibliographies. ●Item 831-C-8 S/N 017-024-01250-5 @ GPO $6.50

1. Drug abuse — Prevention — United States. I. Jones, Coryl LaRue. II. Battjes, Robert. III. National Institute on Drug Abuse. IV. Series. V. Series: NIDA research monograph ; 56. VI. Series: NIDA research monograph. A RAUS review report. [DNLM 1. Substance Abuse — etiology 2. Substance Abuse — prevention & control — United States] OCLC 12352898

86-499

HE 20.8216:61

Cocaine use in America : epidemiologic and clinical perspectives / editors, Nicholas J. Kozel, Edgar H. Adams. — Rockville, Md. : U.S. Dept.of Health and Human Services, Public Health Service, Alcohol, Drug Abuse, and Mental Health Administration, National Institute on Drug Abuse ; Washington, D.C. : For sale by the Supt. of Docs., U.S. G.P.O., 1985.

viii, 232 p. : ill. ; 24 cm. — (NIDA research monograph ; 61) (DHHS publication ; no. (ADM) 85-1414) Shipping list no.: 85-845-P. Includes bibliographies. ●Item 831-C-8 S/N 017-024-01258-1 @ GPO $5.00

1. Cocaine habit — United States. 2. Cocaine. I. Kozel, Nicholas J. II. Adams, Edgar H. (Edgar Harvey), 1940- III. National Institute on Drug Abuse. IV. Series. V. Series. OCLC 12636797

Figure 2. Part of sample page from the *Monthly Catalog.*

Subject Index 1986

Drug abuse — United States.

Alcohol, drug abuse, and mental health amendments of 1986 : report (to accompany H.R. 5259) (including cost estimate of the Congressional Budget Office)., 86-19970

The clandestine manufacture of illicit drugs : hearings before a subcommittee of the Committee on Government Operations, House of Representatives, Ninety-ninth Congress, first session, September 24, and December 5, 1985., 86-13634

Cocaine abuse and the federal response : hearing before the Select Committee on Narcotics Abuse and Control, House of Representatives, Ninety-ninth Congress, first session, Tuesday, July 16, 1985., 86-17822

Coordinating and expanding services for the prevention, identification and treatment of alcohol and drug abuse among Indian youth, and for other purposes : report (to accompany S. 1298)., 86-9021 ——entry no.

Drug abuse in the military : hearing before the Subcommittee on Children, Family, Drugs, and Alcoholism of the Committee on Labor and Human Resources, United States Senate, Ninety-ninth Congress, first session, on reviewing the problem of drug abuse in the military, June 27, 1985., 86-2038

Drug use before and during drug abuse treatment : 1979-1981 TOPS admission cohorts /, 86-500

Drugs and dropouts : a report of the Select Committee on Narcotics Abuse and Control, Ninety-ninth Congress, second session., 86-13681

Drugs of abuse : a supervisor's guide /, 86-6045

The Illicit drug situation in the United States and Canada., 86-1421

Neuroscience methods in drug abuse research /, 86-4342

Subject Index 1987

Drug abuse — United States.

Addiction careers : summary of studies based on the DARP 12-year followup. (HE 20.8217/3:Ad 2/2), 87-2201

The crack cocaine crisis : joint hearing before the Select Committee on Narcotics Abuse and Control, House of Representatives and the Select Committee on Children, Youth, and Families, House of Representatives, Ninety-ninth Congress, second session, Tuesday, July 15, 1986. United States. Congress. House. Select Committee on Narcotics Abuse and Control. (Y 4.N 16:99-2-15), 87-13493

Dealing with drugs and alcohol in the rail and airline industries : hearing before a subcommittee of the Committee on Government Operations, House of Representatives, One hundredth Congress, first session, February 19, 1987. United States. Congress. House. Committee on Government Operations. Government Activities and Transportation Subcommittee. (Y 4.G 74/7:D 84/ —documents class no. 22), 87-13475——————— entry no.

Drug abuse in the workplace : hearing before the Select Committee on Narcotics Abuse and Control, House of Representatives, Ninety-ninth Congress, second session, May 7, 1986. United States. Congress. House. Select Committee on Narcotics Abuse and Control. (Y 4.N 16:99-2-10), 87-6775

Drug and Alcohol Dependent Offenders Treatment Act of 1986 : report (to accompany H.R. 5076) (including cost estimate of the Congressional Budget Office). United States. Congress. House. Committee on the Judiciary. (Y 1.1/8:99-844), 87-2821

Employee drug testing policies in police departments / McEwen, J. Thomas. (J 28.24:D 84/4), 87-14485

Figure 3. Examples from the Subject Index. Column on the left is from the 1986 index. Column on the right is from 1987 index; note that documents class number has been added.

Congressional Information Service

The Congressional Information Service (CIS) indexes the publications of the U.S. Congress in three parts: *Index*, *Abstracts*, and *Legislative Histories*. Here we will discuss just the *Index* and *Abstracts*. The *Index* and *Abstracts* are issued monthly, with annual cumulation and with cumulative indexes every four years.

Index

The *Index* is made up of four sections: Index of Subject and Names, Index of Titles, Index of Bills and Congressional Publications Numbers, and Index of Committee and Subcommittee Chairmen. The largest and most used section is the Index of Subjects and Names. All the examples and exercises given here will be confined to this section of the *Index* and will be referred to as simply "the Index." Once you have mastered this section, you should have no trouble working with the others. Like using the *Monthly Catalog*, using the CIS is a two-step process. First, look up the subject of your research in the Index. Having located a relevant entry, look up the number for that entry in the specified *Abstracts* volume.

Subject Search Example

Congress is becoming increasingly concerned with environmental issues. Suppose your research topic is about some aspect of acid rain on forests. To find this information, look up the subject in the *Four-Year Cumulative Index 1983–1986*. Figure 4 is part of a page from this index.

Abstracts of Documents

To locate the abstract for that document in the specified *Abstracts* volume, turn to the 1985 *Abstracts* and then look up the abstract number (H 441-2) for the document. The volume is arranged in three parts: H (Housing Committee publications), J (Joint Committee publications), and S (Senate Committee publications).

Figure 5 is part of a page from the 1985 *Abstracts* citing the title and a partial abstract of that hearing.

To locate this document on the shelf, you need the documents classification number, which is always preceded by a small circle, e.g.,°Y4.In8/14:98-30.

This is the basic procedure for locating most documents cited in the CIS.

Subject Search Exercise

Using the CIS *Cumulative Index 1983–1986*, find the title and documents classification number of a report examining acid rain problems and control policies in Europe.

Abstracts of Witnesses

For Congressional hearings, in addition to abstracting the hearing as a whole, CIS also abstracts testimony presented by witnesses or witness panels. The names of witnesses and the subject of their testimony are all cited in the Index. As a searching aid, each abstract is given a decimal number: S181-35.1, S181-35.2, etc. The example in figure 6 shows eleven abstracts of testimonies given by witnesses. Suppose you are still researching the topic acid rain. Looking under *acid rain* in the 1983–1986 *Cumulative Index*, you find the number (84) S181-35.9, a reference to the testimony by William D. Ruckelshaus. To locate this testimony, you must note the paging (p. 293–504), then go back to the base accession number (S181-35) where you will find the title and the documents class number.

Identifying the hearing in the example we have just looked at may seem quite obvious. Certain hearings, however, can have more than 20 decimal numbers, the testimonies all being part of the same hearing. To identify and locate any hearing, you must always go back to the base accession number.

Subject Search Exercise

Using the CIS *Cumulative Index 1983–1986*, locate the testimony that concerned EPA programs appropriations for acid rain control covering the FY (fiscal year) 1986 and answer the following:

1. Names of the two witnesses giving testimony
2. Page references for that testimony
3. Documents classification number for document containing that testimony.

All the publications indexed in CIS are also available on microfiche. For libraries that have these documents only on microfiche, the microfiche copy of the document will be filed under the accession number. Figure 7 is a sample page from the 1985 *Abstracts*, shown as figure 5 in the discussion of the CIS. To locate the microfiche copy of this document, you need the accession number (H441-2) not the documents classification number (°Y4.In8/14:98:30).

Index of Subjects and Names

Acid rain
  Acid rain control program estab,
    84 H361–58, **84** H361–59, **85** H361–4,
    85 H361–5, **85** H361–6, **86** H361–53,
    86 H361–54, **86** H361–55
  Acid rain control program estab, bill texts,
    84 S322–10
  Acid rain control regulatory options, CBO
    analysis, **86** J932–21
  Acid rain effects on forests, **85** H441–2
  Acid rain mitigation technologies and policy
    issues, **83** H702–21
  Acid rain problems and control,
    84 H701–48, **84** S312–7, **84** S321–12,
    84 S321–22
  Acid rain problems and control policies in
    Europe, congressional study mission rpt,
    85 H362–7
  "Acid Rain Related Research: Adequacy of
    High-Sulfur Coal Research and the
    Current of the Technology",
    84 S401–24.1
  Acid rain research programs oversight and
    acid rain control proposals, **85** S311–13
  Acid rain sources, impact, and mitigation
    strategies, **84** H362–9
  Air pollution and acid rain problems in natl
    parks, **86** H441–15
  Air pollution effects on forests, Forest
    Service research program estab,
    85 H443–43, **86** H163–10
  Alzheimer's disease impact and causes,
    84 H141–3
  Clean Air Act programs, extension and
    revision, **84** S321–11
  Clean Air Act programs, FY85-FY89
    authorization, **84** S323–2
  Coal-fired electric power plants emission
    reduction technology R&D status,
    85 H361–79.4
  Coal industry status and prospects, pollution
    control, and R&D programs, **85** H361–29

1985 *Abstract* in which this document is abstracted

accession no.

Figure 4. Part of sample page from *Four-year Cumulative Index 1983-1986.*

title

accession no. ——— **H441-2**   **EFFECTS OF AIR POLLUTION AND ACID RAIN ON FOREST DECLINE.**
June 7, 1984.   98-2.
iv+230 p. il.   † CIS/MF/5
•Item 1023-A; 1023-B.

documents class no. ——————— °Y4.In8/14:98-30.
MC 85-3933.   LC 84-603823.

Committee Serial No. 98-30. Hearing before the *Subcom on Mining, Forest Management, and Bonneville Power Administration* to examine the effects of air pollution on forest growth and production.

Appendix (p. 49-230) includes submitted statements, correspondence, witnesses' written statements, and:

- Backiel, Adela (CRS), "Acid Rain: Does It Contribute to Forest Decline?" updated version, May 29, 1984 (p. 221- 225).

H441-2.1: June 7, 1984. p. 4-18.

Witnesses: **BUCKMAN, Robert E.,** Dep Chief, Research, Forest Service.
SHEA, Keith R., Assoc Dep Chief; representing the Interagency Task Force on Acid Precipitation.

Statements and Discussion: Review of research on acid rain impact on forests; lack of evidence to attribute decline in tree diameter growth to acid rain.

H441-2.2: June 7, 1984. p. 18-29, 69-140.

Witness: **RIEDERER von PAAR, Franz,** chief forester, Prince of Thurn and Taxis Admin; pres, German Forestry Assn.

Statement and Discussion: Nature and extent of forest damage due to air pollution in West Germany (related rpt, p. 84-88).

Insertion:

- Scholz, Florian, "Report on Effects of Acidifying and Other Air Pollutants on Forests" prepared for UN Economic Commission for Europe, Apr. 1984, with tables, graphs, and diagrams (p. 89-140).

Figure 5. Part of sample page from the 1985 *Abstracts.* Copyright 1986 by Congressional Information Service, Inc. All rights reserved.

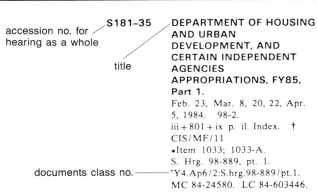

accession no. for hearing as a whole

title

documents class no.

S181–35

DEPARTMENT OF HOUSING AND URBAN DEVELOPMENT, AND CERTAIN INDEPENDENT AGENCIES APPROPRIATIONS, FY85, Part 1.
Feb. 23, Mar. 8, 20, 22, Apr. 5, 1984. 98-2.
iii + 801 + ix p. il. Index. †
CIS/MF/11
•Item 1033; 1033-A.
S. Hrg. 98-889, pt. 1.
°Y4.Ap6/2:S.hrg.98-889/pt.1.
MC 84-24580. LC 84-603446.

Hearings before the *Subcom on HUD and Independent Agencies Appropriations* to consider FY85 budget requests for HUD and related agencies.
Includes a subject index, by agency (p. v-ix).

S181–35.1: Feb. 23, 1984. p. 1-10.
Witness: **ADAMS, Andrew J. (Gen.),** Sec, Amer Battle Monuments Commission (ABMC).
Budget Explanation: ABMC request for FY85 for maintenance of U.S. military monuments and cemeteries abroad and certain memorials in the U.S.

S181–35.2: Feb. 23, 1984. p. 11-25.
Witness: **GLEASON, Joseph E. (Col.),** Dir, Casualty and Memorial Aff, Office of the Adjutant Gen, Army Dept.
Budget Explanation: Army Dept FY85 request for operation and maintenance of Arlington and Soldiers Home National Cemeteries, and for continuing construction and development at Arlington.

S181–35.3: Feb. 23, 1984. p. 27-43.
Witness: **KNAUER, Virginia H.,** Spec Adviser to the Pres; Dir, US Office of Consumer Aff (USOCA).
Budget Explanation: USOCA request for FY85 for consumer programs, including information programs and representation of consumer interests in certain interagency regulatory proceedings.

S181–35.4: Feb. 23, 1984. p. 45-74.
Witness: **NASIF, Teresa N.,** Dir, Consumer Info Center (CIC).
Budget Explanation: CIC request for FY85 to encourage production, dissemination, and public awareness of consumer information published by Federal departments and agencies.

S181–35.5: Mar. 8, 1984. p. 75-111.
Witness: **TURNAGE, Thomas K.,** Dir, Selective Service System.

S181–35.6: Mar. 8, 1984. p. 113-219.
Witnesses: **STEORTS, Nancy H.,** Chm, Consumer Product Safety Commission (CPSC). **SCANLON, Terrence M.,** Vice Chm. **STATLER, Stuart M. ARMSTRONG, Saundra B.,** both Commrs.
Budget Explanation: CPSC request for FY85 for hazard identification and analysis, engineering and sciences, information and education, and compliance and enforcement activities related to injurious consumer products.

S181–35.7: Mar. 8, 1984. p. 221-254.
Witness: **KEYWORTH, George A., II,** Science Adviser to Pres; Dir, OSTP.
Budget Explanation: OSTP request for FY85 for assistance to the President in science and technology policy, review of Federal R&D budgets, advice to the National Security Council on scientific and technological factors related to national security and international issues, and coordination of Federal R&D programs.

S181–35.8: Mar. 20, 1984. p. 255-292.
Witness: **HILL, A. Alan,** Chm, CEQ; Dir, Office of Environmental Quality.
Budget Explanation: CEQ request for FY85 for environmental policy analysis and development, interagency coordination of environmental quality programs, and environmental data acquisition and assessment.
Insertion:
– CEQ worst case analysis requirements for environmental impact statements, Federal, State, local, and public comments on Aug. 1983 draft regulations, excerpts (p. 268-277).

accession no. for individual testimony

S181–35.9: Mar. 20, 1984. p. 293-504.
Witness: **RUCKELSHAUS, William D.,** Administrator, EPA.
Budget Explanation: EPA request for FY85 for:
a. R&D, pollution abatement and control, and enforcement programs, including aid to States and localities relating to air and water quality, drinking water, hazardous waste management, pesticides, radiation, interdisciplinary environmental activities, and toxic substances.
b. Acid rain R&D program.
c. Management and support activities, buildings and facilities, and construction grants.
d. Hazardous Substance Response Trust Fund (Superfund) R&D, enforcement, and management activities.

Supplemental FY84 request for acid rain R&D, and for Superfund activities.

Figure 6. Part of sample page from 1984 *Abstracts* showing individual testimony.

accession no. ——— **H441-2** **EFFECTS OF AIR POLLUTION AND ACID RAIN ON FOREST DECLINE.**
June 7, 1984. 98-2.
iv+230 p. il. † CIS/MF/5
•Item 1023-A; 1023-B.
°Y4.In8/14:98-30.
MC 85-3933. LC 84-603823.

Committee Serial No. 98-30. Hearing before the *Subcom on Mining, Forest Management, and Bonneville Power Administration* to examine the effects of air pollution on forest growth and production.

Appendix (p. 49-230) includes submitted statements, correspondence, witnesses' written statements, and:

- Backiel, Adela (CRS), "Acid Rain: Does It Contribute to Forest Decline?" updated version, May 29, 1984 (p. 221- 225).

H441-2.1: June 7, 1984. p. 4-18.

Witnesses: **BUCKMAN, Robert E.,** Dep Chief, Research, Forest Service.
SHEA, Keith R., Assoc Dep Chief; representing the Interagency Task Force on Acid Precipitation.

Statements and Discussion: Review of research on acid rain impact on forests; lack of evidence to attribute decline in tree diameter growth to acid rain.

H441-2.2: June 7, 1984. p. 18-29, 69-140.

Witness: **RIEDERER von PAAR, Franz,** chief forester, Prince of Thurn and Taxis Admin; pres, German Forestry Assn.

Statement and Discussion: Nature and extent of forest damage due to air pollution in West Germany (related rpt, p. 84-88).

Insertion:

- Scholz, Florian, "Report on Effects of Acidifying and Other Air Pollutants on Forests" prepared for UN Economic Commission for Europe, Apr. 1984, with tables, graphs, and diagrams (p. 89-140).

Figure 7. Part of sample page from the 1985 *Abstracts.* Copyright 1986 by Congressional Information Service, Inc. All rights reserved.

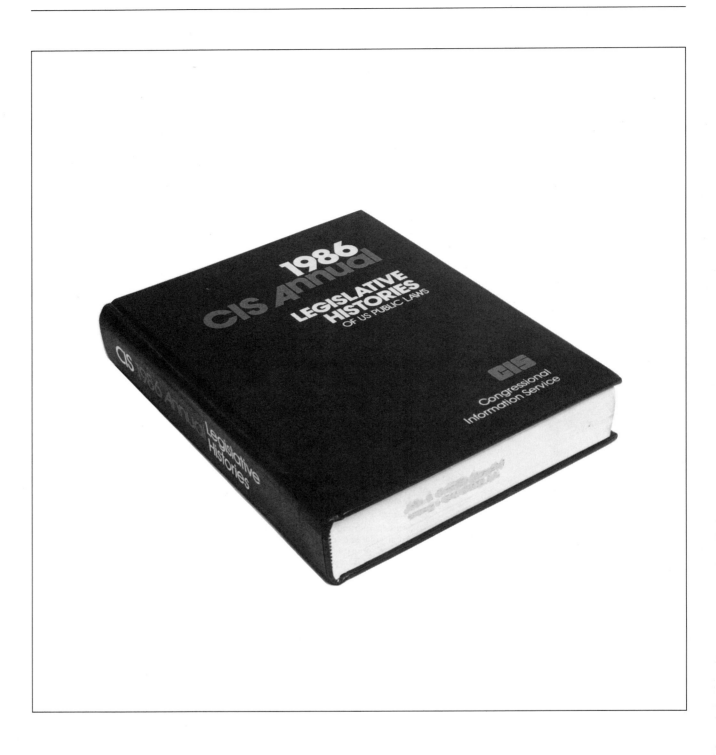

Legislative Histories of U.S. Public Laws

The CIS *Index* and *Abstracts* cover the publications issued by Congress. The CIS *Legislative Histories of U.S. Public Laws* abstracts the public laws published by the Federal Register Office. Issued annually, *Legislative Histories* cites basically all the laws enacted during a particular year or Congressional session. In addition, it cites all documents relevant to a specific law from current and preceding Congresses. In other words, it is a comprehensive record of the entire history of a law, which frequently can be traced back through several Congresses. This record provides an advantage over the abstracts where tracing legislation can often be tedious, each volume of the abstracts covering just one Congressional session.

Subject Search Example

For a sample search in the 1986 *Legislative Histories*, take as an example the new immigration reform law, one of the most publicized laws of 1986. First, look in the Subject and Names Index at the back of the *Legislative Histories* to find the PL (public law) number, then look up that number in the Abstracts section of the *Legislative Histories*. The first item given in the abstracts is always the abstract of the law itself and is numbered 1.1. See sample page shown in figure 8.

As an organization aid, all legislative histories—that is, all documents relevant to a particular law—are organized and numbered by categories of publications. The categories are numbered in the text as follows:

1. Public law (see sample shown in figure 8)
2. Reports
3. Bills
4. Debate
5. Hearings
6. Committee prints
7. Documents
8. Miscellaneous

Partial citations covering the first four categories are given in figure 9 for the Immigration Reform and Control Act, Public Law 99-603.

Subject Search Exercise

Of the laws enacted by the 99th Congress, the one having probably the greatest effect on the nation was the Tax Reform Act of 1986. Using the 1986 *Legislative Histories*, answer the following:

1. The income tax reform proposal resulted in the Tax Reform Act of 1986. What is the public law number for this act?
2. Looking under Bills (category 3), for the 99th Congress, what is the number of the enacted House bill (abbreviated H.R.)?
3. When was the bill passed by the House?
4. When was it passed by the Senate?

public law no.

Public Law 99-603

100 Stat. 3359

Immigration Reform and Control Act of 1986

November 6, 1986

Public Law

1.1   Public Law 99-603, approved Nov. 6, 1986. (S. 1200)

(CIS86:PL99-603   87 p.)

"To amend the Immigration and Nationality Act to revise and reform the immigration laws, and for other purposes."

Amends the Immigration and Nationality Act to reduce illegal immigration and revise immigration policy and procedures.

Establishes civil and criminal penalties for the knowing employment or recruitment of illegal aliens. Defers enforcement of penalties for employment of seasonal agricultural workers and makes conforming amendments to the Migrant and Seasonal Agricultural Worker Protection Act.

Prohibits employment discrimination based on national origin or citizenship status and establishes civil penalties for violations.

Requires feasibility studies on systems for verifying the work eligibility status of legal aliens and on production of counterfeit-resistant social security cards.

Revises criminal penalties for fraud or misuse of entry or identification documents.

P.L. 99-603 Reports

92nd Congress

2.1   H. Rpt. 92-1366 on H.R. 16188, "Amending the Immigration and Nationality Act," Aug. 17, 1972.

(CIS72:H523-23   15 p.)

Recommends passage with amendments of H.R. 16188, to amend the Immigration and Nationality Act to make it unlawful knowingly to hire aliens who have not been lawfully admitted for permanent residence or are not authorized by the Attorney General to work, and to establish a procedure for the imposition of sanctions against employers who hire illegal aliens.

H.R. 16188 is a clean version of H.R. 14831. Includes individual views (p. 15).

93rd Congress

Figure 8. Part of sample page from the Abstracts section of 1986 *Legislative Histories.* Copyright 1987 by Congressional Information Service, Inc. All rights reserved.

categories 1, 2, 3, 4

Public Law

1.1 **Public Law 99-603, approved Nov. 6, 1986. (S. 1200)**

(CIS86:PL99-603   87 p.)

"To amend the Immigration and Nationality Act to revise and reform the immigration laws, and for other purposes."
Amends the Immigration and Nationality Act to reduce illegal immigration and revise immigration policy and procedures.
Establishes civil and criminal penalties for the knowing employment or recruitment of illegal aliens. Defers enforcement of penalties for employment of seasonal agricultural workers and makes conforming amendments to the Migrant and Seasonal Agricultural Worker Protection Act.
Prohibits employment discrimination based on national origin or citizenship status and establishes civil penalties for violations.

P.L. 99-603 Reports

92nd Congress

2.1 **H. Rpt. 92-1366 on H.R. 16188, "Amending the Immigration and Nationality Act," Aug. 17, 1972.**

(CIS72:H523-23   15 p.)

Recommends passage with amendments of H.R. 16188, to amend the Immigration and Nationality Act to make it unlawful knowingly to hire aliens who have not been lawfully admitted for permanent residence or are not authorized by the Attorney General to work, and to establish a procedure for the imposition of sanctions against employers who hire illegal aliens.
    H.R. 16188 is a clean version of H.R. 14831. Includes individual views

P.L. 99-603 Bills

92nd Congress

HOUSE BILLS

3.1 **H.R. 14831 as introduced.**

3.2 **H.R. 16188 as introduced Aug. 3, 1972; as reported by the House Judiciary Committee Aug. 17, 1972; as passed by the House Sept. 12, 1972.**

93rd Congress

P.L. 99-603 Debate

118 Congressional Record
92nd Congress, 2nd Session - 1972

4.1 **Sept. 12, House consideration and passage of H.R. 16188, p. 30153-86.**

119 Congressional Record
93rd Congress, 1st Session - 1973

4.2 **May 3, House consideration and passage of H.R. 982, p. 14179-209.**

Figure 9. Part of sample pages from the 1986 *Legislative Histories* pointing out category numbers. Copyright 1987 by Congressional Information Service, Inc. All rights reserved.

Congressional Record Index

Name and Subject

The *Congressional Record* covers basically the proceedings and debates of Congress. The *Record* actually includes a lot more than that but there is no need to go into a full explanation of the *Record* here.

There are two editions of the *Record*, the daily *Record*, which appears on the morning after the day to which it relates, and the bound *Record*, which appears sometime in the following year in volumes numbered as they are published. The examples and exercises given here are confined to the daily edition, that being the most sought after for any recent Congressional deliberations.

The *Congressional Record Index* is the key to the contents of the daily *Record*. Indexed by name and subject, it leans heavily toward legislative action and remarks by members of Congress. It is issued biweekly; unfortunately there is no cumulative index.

Subject Search Example

To locate a specific text in the *Record*, you will need the page reference and the date given after each entry. The *Record* is divided into four sections, with separate paging sequence for each section: House (H), Senate (S), Extension of Remarks (E), and Daily Digest (D).

Suppose, for example, your topic is on the Iraqi attack on the U.S.S. *Stark*. Figure 10 is part of a sample page from the *Index* of June 1–12, 1987. If you wanted to read "Remarks in Senate" on the Iraqi missile attack, you would look up page S7495 in the June 2 issue of the *Record*.

Figure 11 is part of page S7495 from the June 2 issue of the *Record*.

Subject Search Exercise

"Remarks in House" recorded reaction on the withdrawal of sales of Maverick missiles to Saudi Arabia. Using the *Congressional Record Index*, June 1–12, 1987, answer the following:

1. Page reference and issue of the *Record* containing this address.
2. Name of Congressman giving this address.

History of Bills and Resolutions

The *Congressional Record Index* contains another section at the back, History of Bills and Resolutions. Although the *Index* is not cumulative, the references to bills in the History section are cumulative, so that the latest index giving reference to a bill shows the entire history for the session.

Subject Search Example

Taking S. (Senate bill) 903 as an example, figure 12 is a sample page from the History of the June 1–12 Index showing all references to S. 903 as it proceeds through both houses, is finally signed by the President, and becomes a public law. The abstract of the law could then be looked up in the CIS 1987 *Legislative Histories* under its number (Public Law 100-41).

In this section page numbers are not identified by date. To locate the date for the last page reference (S7447), look at the list of dates and pages included in index on the first page of the Index. (See figure 13.) To locate dates from other pages, consult this list in previous indexes. Since there has already been an exercise on the Index, no exercise will be provided for the History of Bills and Resolutions.

CONGRESSIONAL RECORD INDEX 171

STATES

STALLINGS, RICHARD H. *(a Representative from Idaho)*
Bills and resolutions introduced by, as cosponsor
Agriculture: Farm Credit System reserve for bad debts (see H.R. 2603), H4261 [4JN]
————job training for transition to other economic activities (see H.R. 1202), H4325 [9JN]
————price support loan rates for the 1987 crop of corn and the 1988 crop of wheat (see H.R. 2610), H4559 [11JN]
Baltic Freedom Day: designate (see H.J. Res. 159), H4466 [10JN]
Benign Essential Blepharospasm Awareness Week: designate (see H.J. Res. 224), H4199 [3JN]
Consolidated Farm and Rural Development Act: loans to farmers and ranchers (see H.R. 2576), H4559 [11JN]
Dept. of Defense: prohibit upgrading of Maverick missiles for Saudi Arabia (see H.J. Res. 302), H4560 [11JN]
Emergency Medical Services Week: designate (see H.J. Res. 134), H4560 [11JN]
Federal employees: conduct study on annuities, personnel management, and individual retirement planning (see H.R. 388), H4559 [11JN]
Hamadei, Mohammed: extradition for murder trial (see H. Con. Res. 94), H4076 [1JN]
Remarks by, on
Peregrine falcon: preservation, E2212• [2JN]
STANCZYK, STANLEY
Remarks in House
Tribute, E2283 [8JN]
STANGELAND, ARLAN *(a Representative from Minnesota)*
Bills and resolutions introduced by, as cosponsor
Baltic Freedom Day: designate (see H.J. Res. 159), H4560 [11JN]
Foreign countries: assistance of international financial institutions for production of commodities and minerals in surplus (see H.R. 306), H4465

Public lands: restrictions on land use in national parks and monuments (see H.R. 1173), H4325 [9JN]
Wilbur J. Cohen Federal Building: designate (see H.R. 2655), H4464 [10JN]
Remarks by, on
Congressional Record: revise and extend remarks, H4068 [1JN]
Medicare and Medicaid Patient and Program Protection Act: enact (H.R. 1444), H4061, H4066-H4063 [1JN]
Petroleum: surcharge on imports to compensate for cost of U.S. protection of Persian Gulf shipping (H.R. 2579), H4114• [2JN]
Social Security Act: amend title XVIII (H.R. 2470), H4174• [3JN]
Remarks in House relative to
Special order: granted, H4127 [2JN], H4197 [3JN]
STARK (U.S.S.)
Articles and editorials
240 Women Aboard Tender in Bahrain, S7613 [4JN]
Letters
Iraqi missile attack: Caspar W. Weinberger, Sec. of Defense, H4327 [10JN]
————James and Margaret Keck, S7495 [2JN]
Readiness: sailor killed on board, H4107 [2JN]
To father: Lloyd A. Wilson, H4079 [2JN]
Remarks in House
Iraq: missile attack, H4079 [2JN], H4327 [10JN], E2208 [2JN]
Wilson, Lloyd A.: tribute, H4079 [2JN]
Remarks in Senate
Iraq: missile attack, S7495 [2JN]
Statements
Military Assistance: Saudi Arabia, S7535 [3JN]
STATES
Analyses

Figure 10. Part of page from *Congressional Record Index* showing entry for U.S.S. *Stark*.

June 2, 1987 — remarks in Senate on Iraqi missile attack — CONGRESSIONAL RECORD — SENATE   S 7495

staff began to work with the school systems of the city and counties to incorporate material about burn prevention into the school curriculum. Formal pretesting and posttesting and statistical methodology for evaluation of this program were designed by the Johns Hopkins School of Public Health. After only 1 year, the awareness of the hazards of burning have dramatically increased among these targeted school children. This effort is now being expanded to the elderly and to the work force.

Mr. President, the problem of burn injury in America is a tragic one. Every 4 years, as many Americans die because of burns as were killed in the entire Vietnam war. Two million people are burned each year, and 50,000 of those are permanently disabled. Fire particularly threatens the young; 20 percent of those killed by fire in Maryland were less than 7 years old. Many of those who survive must live with heartrending disfigurement. We are fortunate in Maryland to have an institution dedicated to the care of severely burned individuals. The Baltimore Burn Center which serves as a model for the entire Nation.●

WIC

● Mr. D'AMATO. Mr. President, I rise today as a cosponsor of Senate Joint Resoluton 99 which expresses the sense of the Congress that the Special Supplemental Food Program for Women, Infants, and Children [WIC] should receive increasing amounts of appropriations in fiscal year 1988 and succeeding fiscal years.

I am very concerned about the well-being of our Nation's youth. They are this Nation's most precious resource. We can ill-afford to ignore their proper development. The WIC Program is essential in providing its participants with a proper nutritional diet.

WIC is one of the Federal Government's most successful and cost-effective programs. It provides for the nutritional needs of low-income pregnant, breast-feeding, and postpartum, women, infants, and preschool chil-

I would like to commend the distinguished Senator from Arizona in introducing this timely and worthwhile resolution and urge its speedy passage.●

THE "STARK" LESSON AND STAR WARS

● Mr. KERRY. Mr. President, I recently received a letter from two constituents of mine, James and Margaret Keck, who live in Andover, MA. As they suggest, the strategic lesson to be learned from the U.S.S. *Stark* tragedy is the grim fact that technologically advanced defense systems are never as reliable as we would like to believe they are. It is unwise and even dangerous to expect that any military program, let alone star wars, can protect itself against the failures that plague all complex technologies, great or small. I ask for the Keck's letter to be printed in the RECORD.

The letter follows:

ANDOVER, MA, *May 21, 1987.*

THE "STARK" LESSON

The recent attack by an Exocet missile on the frigate *Stark* provides a dramatic demonstration of some of the many reasons why President Reagan's star wars defense systems is unlikely to work. Any attack will be unexpected, the system will not be on full alert; launch of the weapons will be undetected; they will come in "under the deck of the ship in the clutter of the waves"; a computer will be "down" or will malfunction.

If a U.S. warship equipped with the most modern defense systems cannot defend itself against one or two missiles with well known characteristics in a situation known to be hazardous, what hope is there for defense against a multiple surprise attack by a variety of sophisticated weapons many of which may never have been seen before and which may not even be recognized as threatening?

The expectation that a star wars defense system can be perfected and would function properly when needed is the height of folly. Its only possible virtue is that its development would keep millions of Americans employed—but wouldn't it be far better if these same millions could be put to work on the problems of energy and the environment?

JAMES KECK,
Ford Professor of Engineering, M.I.T.
MARGARET KECK.●

received. The classified annex referred to in the notification is available to Senators at the Foreign Relations Committee.

The notification follows:

DEFENSE SECURITY ASSISTANCE AGENCY,
Washington, DC, May 29, 1987.
In reply refer to: I-00999/87.
Hon. CLAIBORNE PELL,
Chairman, Committee on Foreign Relations,
U.S. Senate, Washington, DC.

DEAR MR. CHAIRMAN: Pursuant to the reporting requirements of Section 36(b)(5)(C) of the Arms Export Control Act, we are forwarding herewith Transmittal No. 87-A and under separate cover the classified annex thereto. This Transmittal concerns the Department of the Air Force's proposed enhancement or upgrade of capability or sensitivity of technology of a defense article previously sold to Saudi Arabia. The sale was originally notified on certification 84-23 dated 26 January 1984. The estimated net cost of this upgrade is $241 million. Soon after this letter is delivered to your office, we plan to notify the news media of the unclassified portion of this Transmittal.

Sincerely,

PHILIP C. GAST,
Director.

[Transmittal No. 87-A]

NOTICE OF PROPOSED ISSUANCE OF LETTER OF OFFER PURSUANT TO SECTION 36(b)(1) AS PRESCRIBED BY SECTION 36(b)(5)(C) OF THE ARMS EXPORT CONTROL ACT

(i) Prospective Purchaser: Saudi Arabia.
(ii) Total Estimated Value:

	Million
Major defense equipment [1]	$315
Other	45
Total	360

[1] As defined in Section 47(6) of the Arms Export Control Act.

Note.—The estimated net cost of the upgrade is $241 million.

(iii) Description of Articles or Services Offered: Sixteen hundred AGM-65D Maverick missiles are proposed to be sold in lieu of 1,600 AGM-65B Maverick missiles previously notified in transmittal 84-23 dated 26 January 1984. Procurement of the previously approved AGM-65B missiles and related items was held in abeyance at the request of the Saudi Arabian Government. This sale also includes training missiles, spares, support equipment and related logistics support.

(iv) Military Department: Air Force (AFU, Amendment 1).
(v) Sales Commission, Fee, etc., Paid, Of-

Figure 11. Part of the page from the *Congressional Record* referred to in figure 10.

H.B. 4

Senate bill no.

CONGRESSIONAL RECORD INDEX

S. 808—A bill to clarify the application of the Clayton Act with respect to rates, charges, or premiums filed by a title insurance company with State insurance departments or agencies; to the Committee on the Judiciary.
By Mr. McCLURE (for himself, Mr. Kasten, and Mr. Symms), S3616
Cosponsors added, S4878, S7096, S7889

S. 824—A bill to establish clearly a Federal right of action by aliens and United States citizens against persons engaging in torture or extrajudicial killing, and for other purposes; to the Committee on the Judiciary.
By Mr. SPECTER, S3729
Cosponsors added, S7994

S. 831—A bill to provide grants to States for fellowships for individuals who have outstanding ability, demonstrate and interest in a teaching career, and will teach in areas of the State in which there is a shortage of quality elementary or secondary school teachers or in fields of study in which there is a shortage of quality elementary or secondary school teachers, or both, and for other purposes; to the Committee on Labor and Human Resources.
By Mr. BINGAMAN (for himself, Mr. Rockefeller, Mr. Baucus, Mr. Glenn, Mr. Riegle, Mr. Chiles, Mr. Sarbanes, Mr. Kerry, and Mr. Byrd), S3847
Cosponsors added, S4375, S7578

S. 837—A bill to amend the Fair Labor Standards Act of 1938 to restore the minimum wage to a fair and equitable rate. and for other purposes; to the Committee on Labor and Human Resources.
BY Mr. KENNEDY, S3847
Cosponsors added, S7096, S7578

S. 839—A bill to authorize the Secretary of Energy to enter into incentive agreements with certain States and affected Indian tribes concerning the storage and disposal of high-level radioactive waste and spent nuclear fuel, and for other purposes; to the Committee on Energy and Natural Resources.
By Mr. JOHNSTON (for himself and Mr. McClure), S3847

Committee on Commerce, Science, and Transportation.
By Mr. GORE, (for himself, Mr. Ford, Mr. Bumpers, Mr. Pryor, Mr. Sasser, Mr. Rockefeller, Mr. Sanford, and Mr. Cochran), S4289
Cosponsors added, S4375, S4595, S4761, S7490

S. 903—A bill to extend certain protections under title 11 of the United States Code, the Bankruptcy Code; to the Committee on the Judiciary.
By Mr. METZENBAUM (for himself, Mr. Heinz, Mr. Glenn, Mr. Specter, Mr. Byrd, Mr. Rockefeller, Mr. Levin, Mr. Boschwitz, Mr. Shelby, Mr. Bumpers, Mr. Inouye, Ms. Mikulski, Mr. Sarbanes, Mr. Lugar, Mr. Riegle, and Mr. Durenberger), S4466
Reported (no written report), S4988
Passed Senate, S5151
Referred to the Committee on the Judiciary, H2085
Passed House, H2981
Examined and signed in the House, H3062
Examined and signed in the Senate, S5887
Presented to the President, S5887
Approved [Public Law 100–41], S7447

S. 924—A bill to revise the allotment formula for the Alcohol, Drug Abuse, and Mental Health Services Block Grant under part B of title XIX of the Public Health Service Act; to the Committee on Labor and Human Resources.
By Mr. BENTSEN (for himself and Mr. Proxmire), S4628
Cosponsors added, S5765, S7490

S. 927—A bill to protect caves resources on Federal lands, and for other purposes; to the Committee on Energy and Natural Resources.
By Mr. DASCHLE, S4718
Cosponsors added, S6921, S7889

S. 930—A bill to amend the Stevenson-Wydler Technology Innovation Act of 1980 to establish a Center on State and Local Initiatives on Productivity, Technology, and Innovation, and for other purposes; to the Committee on Commerce, Science, and Transportation.
By Mr. BUMPERS, S4718

Passed House, H3546
Examined and signed in the House, H3718
Examined and signed in the Senate, S6735
Presented to the President, S6897
Approved [Public Law 100–47], S7447

S. 950—A bill to establish a specialized corps of judges necessary for certain Federal proceedings required to be conducted, and for other purposes; to the Committee on the Judiciary.
By Mr. HEFLIN (for himself, Mr. Specter, Mr. Shelby, Mr. Durenberger, Mr. Heinz, Mr. Sarbanes, Mr. Sasser, Mr. Gore, and Mr. Sanford), S4853
Cosponsors added, S8066

S. 958—A bill to dedicate the North Cascades National Park to Senator Henry M. Jackson; to the Committee on Energy and Natural Resources.
By Mr. JOHNSTON (for himself, Mr. McClure, Mr. Evans, and Mr. Adams), S4853
Reported (no written report), S7566
Passed Senate, S7776
Cosponsors added, S7889
Referred to the Committee on Interior and Insular Affairs, H4557

S. 962—A bill to amend the Internal Revenue Code of 1986 to allow a credit against tax for expenses incurred in the care of elderly family members; to the Committee on Finance.
By Mr. HEINZ, S4854
Cosponsors added, S6399, S7490, S7682

S. 970—A bill to authorize a research program for the modification of plants focusing on the development and production of new marketable industrial and commercial products, and for other purposes; to the Committee on Agriculture, Nutrition, and Forestry.
By Mr. HARKIN (for himself, Mr. Leahy, Mr. Lugar, and Mr. Glenn), S4988
Cosponsors added, S7994, S8066

S. 982—A bill to authorize payments to States to be used for grants to provide support for family day care providers; to the Committee on Labor and Human Resources.

Figure 12. Part of sample page from History of Bills and Resolutions section of *Congressional Record Index*.

No. XI

Congressional Record Index

PROCEEDINGS AND DEBATES OF THE 100ᵗʰ CONGRESS, FIRST SESSION

Vol. 133   JUNE 1 TO JUNE 12, 1987   *Nos. 87 to 96*

NOTE.—For debate and action on bills and resolutions see "History of Bills and Resolutions" at end of Index, under numbers referred to in Index entry.

DATES AND PAGES INCLUDED IN INDEX XI

June 1	....	H4059–H4076	E2157–E2173	D747–D750
June 2	S7389–S7515	H4077–H4131	E2175–E2213	D751–D758
June 3	S7517–S7591	H4133–H4200	E2215–E2243	D759–D766
June 4	S7593–S7693	H4201–H4263	E2245–E2271	D768–D774
June 5	S7695–S7759			D776–D782
June 8		H4265–H4309	E2273–E2290	D783–D786
June 9	S7761–S7904	H4311–H4326	E2291–E2308	D788–D794
June 10	S7905–S8006	H4327–H4471	E2309–E2340	D796–D802
June 11	S8007–S8091	H4473–H4568	E2341–E2388	D803–D810
June 12		H4569–H4575	E2389–E2391	D811–D816

NOTE: elements in brackets which follow page numbers in the Index refer to the dates of the Congressional Record in which those pages may be found.

A.S.C.E. JOURNAL OF PROFESSIONAL ISSUES IN ENGINEERING
Articles and editorials
 Panama Canal—Its Major Marine Operational Problems and Solution, S7764–S7768 [9JN]
ABDNOR, JAMES *(a former Representative from South Dakota)*
Testimonies
 Committee on Small Business: Small Business Act Amendment to Reform the Capital Ownership Development Program (H.R. 1807), D772 [4JN]

ACID DEPOSITION CONTROL ACT
Bills and resolutions
 Enact (see H.R. 2666)
Remarks in House
 Enact (H.R. 2666), E2375, E2385 [11JN]
Summaries
 Provisions of H.R. 2666, E2376 [11JN]
ACKERMAN, GARY L. *(a Representative from New York)*
Bills and resolutions introduced by, as cosponsor
 Aeronautics: air carrier seating of persons holding

Persian Gulf: cooperation of allies with significant security and economic interests in region (see H. Con. Res. 135), H4307 [8JN]
Postal Service: protect employee rights to participation in political processes (see H.R. 21), H4130 [2JN]
Saudi Arabia: prohibit upgrading of Maverick missiles (see H.J. Res. 302), H4325 [9JN]
Social Security: restore provisions for determining order of payment of lump-sum death benefits (see H.R. 1977), H4130 [2JN]

Figure 13. Part of an opening page of the *Congressional Record Index* showing the dates and pages included in it.

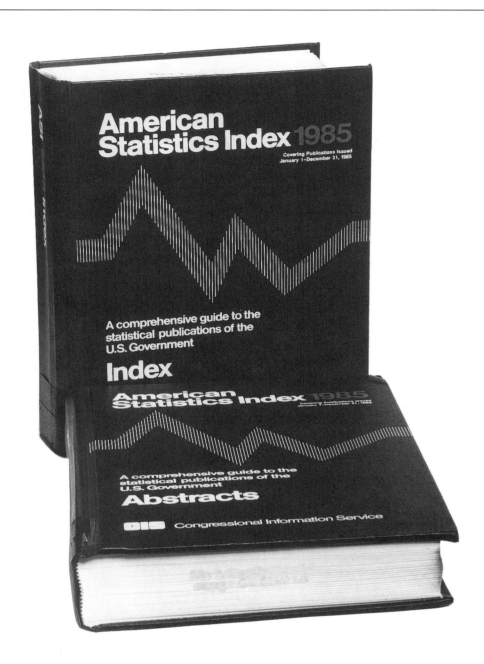

American Statistics Index

Individual and Special Publications

The U.S. government releases more statistical data than does any other country or commercial enterprise in the world. Access to most of this data can be found through the *American Statistics Index* (ASI).

ASI is arranged like CIS, with an index volume and an abstracts volume. The *Index* and *Abstracts* are issued monthly with annual cumulations. The *Index* consists of four sections: Subject and Names Index, Index by Categories, Index by Titles, and Index by Agency Report Numbers. The largest and most used section is the Subject and Names Index. All the examples and exercises given here will be confined to this section of the *Index* and will be referred to as simply the Index. Once you have mastered this section, you should have no trouble using any of the others.

Like using CIS, using ASI is a two-step process. First, look up the subject of your research in the Index. Having located a relevant entry, look up the accession number for that entry in the corresponding abstracts.

Subject Search Example

Suppose the topic of your research paper concerns a comparison of homicide statistics in the Chicago area with those from selected other cities. Using the 1985 ASI Index, what report dealt with this matter? To find this report, you look up the subject, Chicago, in the Index. Figure 14 is part of a sample page from the Index.

Now look up the accession number (6068-196) in the *Abstracts*. Figure 15 is part of a sample page from the 1985 ASI *Abstracts* citing the title and the abstract of that report. Notice that the abstract cites Chicago and the other cities involved in the study.

To locate this document on the shelf, you need the documents classification number, which is always preceded by a small circle. What you have just done in this exercise is the basic procedure for locating most documents through ASI.

Subject Search Exercise

Using the 1985 ASI, find a report giving the results of police response to crimes in San Diego and answer the following:

1. Title of the report
2. Documents classification number for that report.

Annuals

ASI indexes mainly four types of publications: annuals and biennials; current periodicals; publications in series; and individual, special, and irregular publications. In many cases ASI describes these publications by giving a main abstract, followed by subordinate abstracts called analytics. The analytics are identified by decimal numbers (.1, .2, .3, etc.) following the main abstract. The following examples will show ASI's methods of handling analytics for these various types of publications.

The example in figure 16 illustrates ASI's analysis of an annual publication. Note that the main abstract is given first, followed by the analytics (subordinate abstracts). If the Index led you to 6824-1.3, to locate the document containing this data, you must go back to the base number (6824-1) where you will find the title and class number of the document.

Periodicals

For periodicals, ASI gives first a main abstract describing the general contents of the periodical, followed by analytics (subordinate abstracts) for the articles in each issue. The example in figure 17 cites a sampling of abstracts for the periodical *Public Health Reports*. If the Index led you to the article "Drugs in Fatally Injured Young Male Drivers" (4042-3.503), to locate the article you must identify the periodical issue (vol. 100, no. 1) and then go back to the base number (4042-3) to find the title and class number of the periodical.

Publications in Series

For publications in series and other types of collective studies, the individual reports that make up these series have their own title and documents class number. Note in the example in figure 18 the separate titles and class numbers for each of the reports included in the Vital and Health Statistics Series 1. If the index led you to 4147-1.20: Plan and Operation of the Hispanic Health and Nutrition Examination Survey, the documents class number for this report is cited below the title and, as is always the case, is identified by a small circle on the left.

All the publications indexed in the ASI are also available on microfiche. For libraries that have these documents only on microfiche, the microfiche copy of the document will be filed under the accession number. Figure 19 is a sample page from ASI *Abstracts*, shown as figure 15 in the discussion of the ASI. To locate the microfiche copy of this document, you need the accession number (6068-196) and not the documents classification number (J28.2:H 75). The searching procedure in the indexes will, of course, remain unchanged.

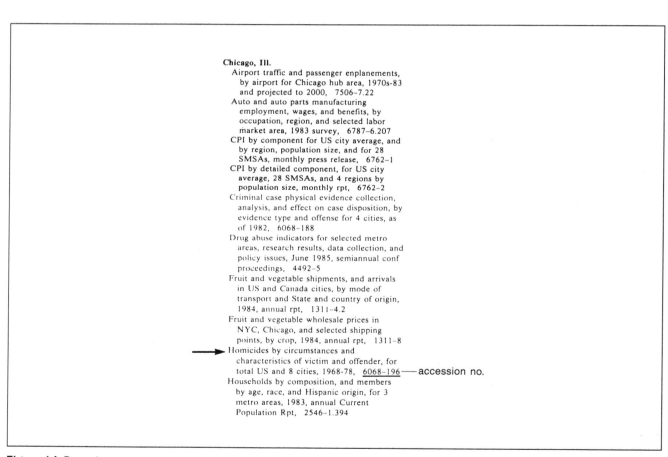

Figure 14. Part of sample page from ASI *Index*. Copyright 1986 by Congressional Information Service, Inc. All rights reserved.

accession no. ———— **6068-196**   **NATURE AND PATTERNS OF AMERICAN HOMICIDE**
May 1985.   x+73 p.
•Item 718-A.   GPO $3.25.
ASI/MF/3
documents _____ S/N 027-000-01228-1.
class no. ———— °J28.2:H75.
MC 85-23332.
LC 85-602207.

By Marc Riedel and Margaret A. Zahn. Report on trends in homicide case characteristics, 1968-78. Data are based on FBI Uniform Crime Reports, and medical examiner and police department records from 8 cities with population over 250,000 and at least 100 homicides in 1978. Report is issued by the National Institute of Justice.

Most data are shown for the U.S. and each of the 8 cities, for homicides involving family members, acquaintances, and strangers. Cities are Philadelphia, Pa.; Newark, N.J.; Chicago, Ill.; St. Louis, Mo.; Memphis, Tenn.; Dallas, Tex.; and Oakland, Calif. The eighth city is listed under a fictitious name because officials there requested anonymity.

Includes 2 charts and 33 tables showing number and rate of homicides, by region; age, sex, and race of victim and offender; presence of narcotics in victim's system at time of death; weapon used; associated felony offense; and location (residence, street, bar, other commercial establishment, other); with selected cross-tabulations.

U.S. data are for 1978 with trends from 1968; data for the 8 cities are for 1978 only.

6068-197   **ROLE OF THE THE GRAND JURY AND THE PRELIMINARY HEARING IN PRETRIAL SCREENING**
1985.   vii+171 p.
•Item 718-A.   GPO $7.00.
ASI/MF/4
S/N 027-000-01230-2.
°J28.2:G76/2.
MC 85-2154.

Figure 15. Part of sample page from ASI *Abstracts*. Copyright 1986 by Congressional Information Service, Inc. All rights reserved.

accession no. ————— 6824–1   **PRODUCTIVITY MEASURES**
for annual   **FOR SELECTED**
                                                          INDUSTRIES, 1954-83
                                                          Annual.   Feb. 1985.
                                                          v + 280 p.   BLS Bull. 2224.
                                                          •Item 768-A-1.   GPO $7.50.
                                                          ASI/MF/5
                                                          S/N 029-001-02833-4.
documents class no. ——— •L2.3:2224.
                                                          MC 85-15432.
                                                                              LC 83-640507.

Annual report presenting productivity indexes
for manufacturing, mining, and selected other industries, annually for various periods, 1954-83.
Data on total and per employee hour output are
derived from statistics compiled by BLS and the
Census Bureau.

Contents:

a. Highlights of trends in output per employee
hour and methodology; with 1 chart and 1
summary table, listed below. (p. 1-8)

b. 133 charts and 244 detailed tables, listed below. (p. 10-277)

c. List of recent BLS publications on productivity and technology. (p. 278-280)

Indexes of output per hour and related measures
for the total private economy or major sectors are
published in *Monthly Labor Review* and *Employment and Earnings* (see 6722-1 and 6742-2,
respectively).

TABLES:
[The following 2 tables are presented for most
industries:

a. Indexes of output per employee hour and output per employee [all, production workers,
nonproduction workers].

b. Indexes of output, employee hours, and employees [all, production workers, nonproduction workers].

For a few industries data are combined on 1 table. Tables present data for 1954-83, unless oth-
erwise noted, and include average annual rates of
change from beginning of series and from 1978
through 1982 or 1983. 1977 = 100.]

6824–1.1: Summary

1. Selected industries: employment, 1983, and
average annual rates of change in output per
employee hour, 1978-83. (p. 5)

6824–1.2: Mining Industries

2-5. Iron mining, crude and usable ore (SIC
1011). (p. 13-15)

6-9. Copper mining, crude ore and recovera-
ble metal (SIC 1021). (p. 17-19)

10-11. Coal mining (SIC 111, 121). (p. 21)

12-13. Bituminous coal and lignite mining
(SIC 121). (p. 23)

14-15. Nonmetallic minerals, except fuels
(SIC 14). (p. 25)

16-17. Crushed and broken stone (SIC 142),
1958-83. (p. 27)

———— accession no. for analytic

6824–1.3: Manufacturing Industries
FOOD AND KINDRED PRODUCTS, TOBACCO

18-19. Red meat products (SIC 2011, 2013),
1967-83. (p. 29)

20-21. Meat packing plants (SIC 2011), 1967-
83. (p. 31)

22-23. Sausages and other prepared meats
(SIC 2013), 1967-83. (p. 33)

24. Fluid milk (SIC 2026), 1958-83. (p. 35)

25-26. Preserved fruits and vegetables (SIC
203), 1954-82. (p. 37)

27-28. Canned fruits and vegetables (SIC
2033), 1958-82. (p. 39)

29-30. Grain mill products (SIC 204), 1963-
81. (p. 41)

Figure 16. Part of sample page from ASI showing both main abstract and analytics.

accession no. for
periodical as
a whole

title of periodical

documents class no.

4042-3

PUBLIC HEALTH REPORTS
Bimonthly. Approx. 110 p.
PHS 85-50193. •Item 497.
GPO: $21.00 per yr; single
copy $5.00. ASI/MF/4
S/N 717-021-00000-2.
°HE20.30:(v.nos.&nos.)
MC 85-957. LC 75-642678.

Bimonthly journal of public health, containing
feature articles, short items, and research reports
on a wide variety of programs and studies. Nov./
Dec. issue contains subject and author indexes
for the year.

Each issue contains:

a. 1-2 editorials by HHS Secretary or other ad-
ministrators.

b. 10-15 articles, including narrative discussions
of public health concerns; and reports on special studies of U.S. and foreign health condi-
tion investigations, health service planning
and evaluation, analysis of vital statistics, and
clinical studies. Issues usually include 2-4 articles focusing on preventive medicine. Many
articles contain references and an abstract.
Those containing statistical material are in-
dividually described below.

c. Letters to the editor.

d. "Programs, Practices, People": short reports
on new programs, studies underway, methods, and grants awarded.

e. "Education Notes": lists of continuing education courses, seminars, and conferences for
public health professionals.

f. List of new Federal and non-Federal publications.

Journal has been published since 1878. Previous
titles include *HSMHA Health Reports* and
Health Service Reports.

Through the Nov./Dec. 1984 issue, report was
described by ASI and microfilmed under 4102-1;
beginning with Jan./Feb. 1985 issue, report is
available on ASI microfiche under this number.

Issues covered during 1985: Jan./Feb.-Nov./
Dec. 1985 (P) (Vol. 100, Nos. 1-6).

January-December 1985

ARTICLES:

JANUARY/FEBRUARY 1985
Vol. 100, No. 1

volume and issue
of periodical

**4042-3.501: Cardiovascular Disease and
Diet: The Public View**

By James T. Heimbach (p. 5-12). Report on
public perceptions of relationship between diet
and cardiovascular disease, based on a 1982
nationwide telephone survey of 4,000 adults.
Includes 8 tables.

**4042-3.502: Cardiovascular Fitness Pro-
gram: Factors Associated with Participation and Adherence**

By Jerrold Mirotznik et al. (p. 13-18). Report
on sociodemographic and health characteristics of persons who participated and did not
participate in fitness programs after being eva-
luated for risk of coronary heart disease.

Based on a 1979 study of 215 clients of the
92nd Street Young Men's-Young Women's
Hebrew Assn Coronary Detection and Inter-
vention Center in NYC. Includes 5 tables
showing regression results.

accession no.
for article

**4042-3.503: Drugs in Fatally Injured
Young Male Drivers**

By Allan F. Williams (p. 19-25). Report on
presence of alcohol, marijuana, and other
drugs in the blood of male drivers killed in
traffic accidents. Based on a 1982-83 study of
440 California males, aged 15-34, who died
within 2 hours of an accident for which they
were judged responsible.

Includes 6 tables showing drivers, by age,
vehicle type, number and type of drugs detect-
ed, and blood alcohol concentration.

**4042-3.504: Estimates of Pregnancies and
Pregnancy Rates for the U.S., 1976-81**

By Stephanie J. Ventura et al. (p. 31-34). Report on number, rate, and outcome of pregnancies, by age and race of mother, selected years
1976-81. Data are from NCHS sources. Includes 2 charts and 2 tables.

Figure 17. Part of pages from ASI. Column on left shows description of *Public Health Reports*; column on right contains abstracts of individual articles. Copyright 1986 by Congressional Information Service, Inc. All rights reserved.

4147-1   PROGRAMS AND COLLECTION PROCEDURES. Vital and Health Statistics Series 1
GPO; for individual bibliographic data, see below.
°HE20.6209:1/(nos.)

Continuing series of reports on NCHS programs and data collection procedures for national statistical surveys, including those based on health interviews, health examinations, and enumerations of hospitals, institutions, and nursing homes.

General report format: introduction describing relationship of a particular data collection program to the entire National Health Survey; narrative sections on survey design, implementation, and data evaluation methods; and appendices, with facsimile survey forms, definitions, and statistical notes.

Reports are described below in order of receipt. Most recent previous report in the series is described in ASI 1982 Annual under this number.

4147-1.18: Inventory of Alcohol, Drug, and Mental Health Data Available from the National Center for Health Statistics
[No. 17.   Apr. 1985. iii + 84 p. PHS 85-1319. °HE20.6209:1/17. •Item 500-E. LC 84-600397. MC 85-25061. S/N 017-022-00870-0. $3.25. ASI/MF/3]

By Charlotte A. Schoenborn. Narrative report describing survey design, basic and mental health-related data elements, data tape availability, and questionnaire source items for NCHS data sets that contain information on mental health and alcohol and drug abuse indicators.

Includes narrative descriptions; lists of indicators, and sociodemographic and other characteristics by which data are tabulated; and facsimile survey form sections for alcohol-related questions; all for individual surveys and data sets.

4147-1.19: National Health Interview Survey Design, 1973-84, and Procedures, 1975-83
[No. 18.   Aug. 1985. iv + 127 p. PHS 85-1320. °HE20.6209:1/18. •Item 500-E. S/N 017-022-00879-3. $4.75. ASI/MF/4]

By Mary G. Kovar and Gail S. Poe. Report examining changes in National Health Interview Survey (NHIS) sample and questionnaire design, estimating and interviewing procedures, and supplements to the basic questionnaire, 1973-84 with some comparisons to earlier surveys.

Includes 3 tables showing sample population and selected results of NHIS surveys using control and experimental questionnaires; and numerous facsimile questionnaire forms.

4147-1.20: Plan and Operation of the Hispanic Health and Nutrition Examination Survey, 1982-84
[No. 19.   Sept. 1985. vi + 429 p. PHS 85-1321. °HE20.6209:1/19. LC 85-010648. S/N 017-022-00893-9. $15.00. ASI/MF/7] — documents class no.

Report on Hispanic Health and Nutrition Examination Survey design and procedures. Survey was conducted July 1982-Dec. 1984.

Includes 2 maps and 10 tables showing sample population and selected survey results, standard errors, and other methodological data; and numerous facsimile questionnaire forms.

Figure 18. Part of a page from ASI showing abstracts of items in a series. Copyright 1986 by Congressional Information Service, Inc. All rights reserved.

accession no. ——— **6068–196** **NATURE AND PATTERNS OF AMERICAN HOMICIDE**
May 1985. x+73 p.
•Item 718-A. GPO $3.25.
ASI/MF/3
S/N 027-000-01228-1.
°J28.2:H75.
MC 85-23332.

LC 85-602207.

By Marc Riedel and Margaret A. Zahn. Report on trends in homicide case characteristics, 1968-78. Data are based on FBI Uniform Crime Reports, and medical examiner and police department records from 8 cities with population over 250,000 and at least 100 homicides in 1978. Report is issued by the National Institute of Justice.

Most data are shown for the U.S. and each of the 8 cities, for homicides involving family members, acquaintances, and strangers. Cities are Philadelphia, Pa.; Newark, N.J.; Chicago, Ill.; St. Louis, Mo.; Memphis, Tenn.; Dallas, Tex.; and Oakland, Calif. The eighth city is listed under a fictitious name because officials there requested anonymity.

Includes 2 charts and 33 tables showing number and rate of homicides, by region; age, sex, and race of victim and offender; presence of narcotics in victim's system at time of death; weapon used; associated felony offense; and location (residence, street, bar, other commercial establishment, other); with selected cross-tabulations.

U.S. data are for 1978 with trends from 1968; data for the 8 cities are for 1978 only.

Figure 19. Part of sample page from ASI *Abstracts*. Copyright 1986 by Congressional Information Service, Inc. All rights reserved.

Index to U.S. Government Periodicals

The *Index to U.S. Government Periodicals* (IUSGP) is an integrated subject and author index to over 180 government periodicals. It is issued quarterly with annual cumulations. The periodicals selected for indexing are those which offer "substantive articles of lasting research and reference value" (introd.).

There are basically three steps in doing a subject search in the IUSGP.

1. Look under the subject in the Index and locate an article.
2. Now note the title of the periodicals, volume number, issue number (if any).
3. Look up the documents class number for that periodical in the list of periodicals indexed at the front of the volume.

Subject Search Example

Suppose that your subject is child abuse and that you want to see the article on child pornography cited on the page shown in figure 20. Having noted the periodical title, volume number, issue number, page number and date, now turn to periodicals indexed list at the front of the volume. It will give you the full periodical title and its classification number. (Copy of a partial list is given in figure 21.)

A sample entry for this reference is given in figure 21 with an explanation of all the bibliographic elements that make up the citation.

Subject Search Exercise

Using the 1985 *Index to U.S. Government Periodicals*, find an article on how spanking a child can be a form of child abuse and answer the following:

1. Author and title of article
2. Title of periodical containing the article
3. Volume number, issue number, and page reference for that article.
4. Documents class number for that periodical.

CHILD abuse
Alabama reaches out. Dorothy Tate and others, Ext Rev
56 3 43 Sum **85-214**
Army Court reexamines excited utterance exception.
Army Law 32 N **85-015**
Child abuse and hearsay. Army Law 39-44 F **85-015** ——— title of article
Child pornography: a worldwide problem. Elliot Abrams, ——— author
periodical title ——— Dept Sta Bul 85 2097 55-56 Ap **85-029**
Claudia Black: children of alcoholics. il Adamha N 11 6 ——— date of issue
volume no. —— 5 Je **85-299**
Defense mechanisms used by sexually abused children.
Christine Adams-Tucker, ref Child Today 14 1 8-12 +
issue no. —— Ja-F **85-022**
Eye of the maelstrom: pretrial preparation of child abuse
page nos. —— cases. James B. Thwing, Army Law 46-66 Je **85-015**
Eye of the malestrom: pretrial preparation of child abuse
cases. James B. Thwing, Army Law 5 25-28 My **85-015**
It shouldn't hurt to be a child. Mark James, Med Bul 42
10-11 4 O-N **85-338**
Justice Department funds Children's Center. Mynda
McGuire, Airman 28 8 7 Ag **84-009**
Medicine in today's trenches: a primer for new Medical
Corps health clinic commanders. Paul E. Whittaker,
ref Med Bul 42 10-11 24-29 O-N **85-338**
Men who murdered: chapter 1. ref FBI Law Enf Bul 54
8 2-6 Ag **85-044**
Pertinence of identity in physical child abuse cases.
Army Law 33 N **85-015**
Professionalism, integrity, cooperation: the wellspring of
law enforcement. William H. Webster, ref, por FBI
Law Enf Bul 54 2 17-20 F **85-044**
Protecting the child witness: avoiding physical
confrontation with the accused. David F. Abernethy,
Army Law 23-31 N **85-015**

Figure 20. Analysis of the elements in a IUSGP citation. Reproduced by permission of Infordata International Inc.

PERIODICALS INDEXED, ABBREVIATIONS and CLASSIFICATION NUMBERS
For addresses and other details, consult the annual index.

ADAMHA N—ADAMHA News, HE20.8013: monthly
Advocate—The Advocate, D108.109: bimonthly
Aging—Aging, HE23.3110: bimonthly
Agric Econ Res—Agricultural Economics Research, A93.26: quarterly
Agric Outl—Agricultural Outlook, A93.10/2: monthly
Agric Res—Agricultural Research, A77.12: 10 issues
Air Def Artil—Air Defense Artillery (continues Air Defense Magazine), D101.77: quarterly × ○
Air F Comp—Air Force Comptroller, D301.73: quarterly
Air F Eng & Serv Q—Air Force Engineering & Services Quarterly, D301.65: quarterly
Air F J Logis—Air Force Journal of Logistics, D301.91: quarterly
Air F Law Rev—Air Force Law Review, D302.9: quarterly
Air Reserv—Air Reservist, D301.8: quarterly
Air Univ Rev—Air University Review, D301.26: bimonthly
Airman—Airman, D301.60: monthly
Alcoh Health & Res W—Alcohol Health and Research World, HE20.8309: quarterly
All Hands—All Hands, D207.17: monthly
Amer Ed—American Education, ED1.10: 10 issues
Amer Rehab—American Rehabilitation, ED1.211: quarterly
Antar Jour US—Antarctic Journal of the United States, NS1.26: quarterly
Appalachia—Appalachia, Y3. Ap 4/2:9-2/bimonthly○
Approach—Approach, D202.13: monthly
Armor—Armor: the Magazine of Mobile Warfare, D101.78/2: bimonthly × ○
Army Commun—Army Communicator, D111.14: quarterly × ○
Army Law—Army Lawyer, D101.22:27-50 monthly
Army Logis—Army Logistician, D101.69: monthly
Army Org Effect—Army Organizational Effectiveness Journal (continues OE Communique), D101.91: quarterly
Army R D & A—Army Research, Development and Acquisition, D101.52/3: bimonthly
Army Reserv—Army Reserve Magazine, D101.43: quarterly
Arts Rev—Arts Review, NF2.11: quarterly
Back Notes—Background Notes on the Countries of the World, S1.123: irregular
Black N Dig—Black News Digest, L1.20/6: weekly × ○
Bul/Bur Just Stat—Bulletin/Bureau of Justice Statistics, J29.11: monthly
Bus Amer—Business America, C61.18: biweekly
C Guard Eng Dig—Coast Guard Engineer's Digest, TD5.17: quarterly
Cancer Treat Rep—Cancer Treatment Reports, HE20.3160: monthly
Child Today—Children Today, HE23.1209: bimonthly
Cong Res Serv Rev—Congressional Research Service Review, LC14.19: 10 issues
Const Rev—Construction Review, C62.10 bimonthly
Crime Lab Dig—Crime Laboratory Digest, J1.4/18: quarterly
Data User N—Data User News, C3.238: monthly
Def Man J—Defense Management Journal, D1.38/2: quarterly
Defense...—Defense..., D2.15/3: monthly   ———documents class no.
→ Dept Sta Bul—Department of State Bulletin, S1.3: monthly
Direction—Direction, D201.17: quarterly
Disab USA—Disabled USA, PrEx1.10/3-2: quarterly
DOE This Month—DOE This Month (continues Energy Insider), E1.54: monthly
Driver—Driver, D301.72: quarterly
Drug Enf—Drug Enforcement, J24.3/2: triannually
Earth Inf Bul—Earthquake Information Bulletin, I19.65: bimonthly
Endang Spec Tech Bul—Endangered Species Technical Bulletin, I49.77: monthly
Energy & Tech Rev—Energy and Technology Review, E1.53: monthly
Eng Update—Engineer Update, D103.69: monthly
Engineer—Engineer, D103.115: quarterly
Engl Teach Forum—English Teaching Forum, IA1.17: quarterly
Env & Water Qual Op Stud—Environment & Water Quality Operational Studies, D103.24/15: irregular × ○
Env Health Persp—Environmental Health Perspectives, HE20.3559: bimonthly
EPA J—EPA Journal, EP1.67: 10 issues
Ext Rev—Extension Review, A43.7: quarterly
FAA Gen Av N—FAA General Aviation News, TD4.9: bimonthly
Faceplate—Faceplate, D211.22: quarterly
Fam Ec Rev—Family Economics Review, A77.708: quarterly
Farm Coop—Farmer Cooperatives, A109.11: monthly
Farmline—Farmline, A93.33/2: monthly
Fathom—Fathom, D202.20: quarterly
FBI Law Enf Bul—FBI Law Enforcement Bulletin, J1.14/8: monthly
FDA Cons—FDA Consumer, HE20.4010: 10 issues

FDA Drug Bul—FDA Drug Bulletin, HE20.4003/3: irregular
● FEC J Elec Admin—FEC Journal of Election Administration, Y3.El2/3:10/ semiannual
FEC Rec—Federal Election Commission Record, Y3.El2/3:11/ monthly
Fed Prob—Federal Probation, Ju10.8: quarterly
Fed Res Bul—Federal Reserve Bulletin, FR1.3: monthly × ○
FEMA NL—Federal Emergency Management Agency Newsletter, FEM1.20: irregular × ○
Fire Man Notes—Fire Management Notes, A13.32: quarterly
Fish & Wild N—Fish and Wildlife News, I49.88: bimonthly
Fish Bul—Fishery Bulletin, C55.313: quarterly
Fly Safe—Flying Safety, D301.44: monthly
Focus: Gr Lakes Water Qual—Focus: On Great Lakes Water Quality, Y3.In8/28:17/ quarterly × ○
FOIA Update—FOIA Update, J1.58: quarterly
Folk C News—Folklife Center News, LC39.10: quarterly
Food & Nutr—Food and Nutrition, A98.11: quarterly
For Agric—Foreign Agriculture, A67.7/2: monthly
Fortitudine—Fortitudine, D214.20: quarterly × ○
Forum—See Engl Teach Forum
GAO Rev—The GAO Review, GA1.15: quarterly
Health Care Fin Rev—Health Care Financing Review, HE22.18: quarterly
Horizons—Horizons S18.58: quarterly
Humanities—Humanities, NF3.11: bimonthly
Hum Devel N—Human Development News, HE23.10: 6 issues
Impact—Impact, Y3.T25:47/ quarterly
Infantry, D102.83: bimonthly
INS Rep—INS Reporter, J21.10/2: quarterly
Intergov Persp—Intergovernmental Perspective, Y3.Ad9/8:11/
J Nat Cancer Inst—Journal of the National Cancer Institute, HE20.3161: monthly
J Rehab Res—Journal of Rehabilitation Research and Development, VA1.23/3: semiannual
J Res Nat Bur Stand—Journal of Research of the National Bureau of Standards, C13.22: bimonthly
JAG Jour—Judge Advocate General (Navy) Journal, D205.7: semiannually
● LBL Res Rev—LBL Research Review, E1.53/2: quarterly
Lib Cong Inf Bul—Library of Congress Information Bulletin, LC1.18: weekly
● Logos-Logos, E1.86/3: triannual
Los Alamos Sci—Los Alamos Science, E1.96: quarterly
MAC Flyer—The MAC Flyer, D301.56: monthly
Maintenance—Maintenance, D301.84: quarterly
Management—Management, PM1.11/2: quarterly
Mar Weath Log—Mariners Weather Log, C55.210: quarterly
Marine Fish Rev—Marine Fisheries Review, C55.310: quarterly
Marines—Marines, D214.24: monthly
Mater & Comp—Materials & Components in Fossil Energy Application, E1.23: bimonthly
Mech—D202.19: bimonthly
Med Bul—Medical Bulletin, D101,42/3: monthly
Med Serv Dig—Medical Service Digest, D304.8: monthly
Mil Chapl Rev—Military Chaplains' Review, D101.22:165-quarterly
Mil Intel—Military Intelligence, D101.84: quarterly
Mil Law Rev—Military Law Review, D101.22:27-100-quarterly
Mil Media Rev—Military Media Review, D101.92: quarterly
Mil Rev—Military Review, D110.7: monthly
Min Bus Today—Minority Business Today, C1.79: quarterly × ○
Mine Safe & H—Mine Safety and Health, L38.9: quarterly
Mon Energy Rev—Monthly Energy Review, E3.9: monthly
Mon Labor Rev—Monthly Labor Review, L2.6: monthly
Monitor—Monitor, E2.19: biweekly
Mosaic—Mosaic, NS1.29: bimonthly
NASA Act—NASA Activities, NAS1.46: monthly
Nav Av News—Naval Aviation News, D202.9: bimonthly
NASA Rep Ed—NASA Report to Educators, NAS1.49: quarterly
Nat Food Rev—National Food Review, A93.16: quarterly
Nav Civ Eng—Navy Civil Engineer, D209.13: quarterly
Nav Res Rev—Naval Research Reviews, D210.11: quarterly
Nav War Col Rev—Naval War College Review, D208.209: bimonthly
Navigator—Navigator, D301.38/4: triannually
New Persp—New Perspectives (formerly Perspectives), CR1.12: quarterly
News & Feat NIH—News & Features from NIH, HE20.3007/2: 10 issues
NOAA—NOAA, C55.14: semiannual
Nuclear Safe—Nuclear Safety, E1.93: quarterly
Occup Outl Q-Occupational Outlook Quarterly, L2.70/4: quarterly
● Ordnance—The Ordnance Magazine, D105.29: quarterly

Figure 21. First part of the list of periodicals indexed in IUSGP. Reproduced by permission of Inlordata International Inc.

Answers to Subject Search Exercises

Using the 1986 Subject Index of the *Monthly Catalog*, find the title and documents classification number of a report covering drug abuse in Canada.

> The illicit drug situation in the United States
> and Canada
> J24.2:D 84/16

Using the *CIS Cumulative Index 1983–1986*, find the title and documents classification number of a report examining acid rain problems and control policies in Europe.

> Acid rain in Europe
> Y4.En 2/3:99-F

Using the *CIS Cumulative Index 1983–1986*, locate the testimony that concerned EPA programs appropriations for acid rain control covering the FY (fiscal year) 1986 and answer the following:

1. Names of the two witnesses giving testimony
   Thomas, Lee M.
   Elkins, Charles L.
2. Page references for that testimony
   p. 1179–1245
3. Documents classification number for document containing that testimony
   Y4.Ap 6/2:S.hrg.99-221/pt.2

Of the laws enacted by the 99th Congress, the one having probably the greatest effect on the nation was the Tax Reform Act of 1986. Using the 1986 *Legislative Histories*, answer the following:

1. The income tax reform proposal resulted in the Tax Reform Act of 1986. What is the public law number for this act?
   P.L. 99-514
2. Looking under Bills (category 3), for the 99th Congress, what is the number of the enacted House bill (abbreviated H.R.)?
   H.R. 3838
3. When was the bill passed by the House?
   Dec. 17, 1985
4. When was it passed by the Senate?
   June 24, 1986

"Remarks in House" recorded reaction on the withdrawal of sales of Maverick missiles to Saudi Arabia. Using the *Congressional Record Index*, June 1–12, 1987, answer the following:

1. Page reference and issue of the *Record* containing this address
   H 4544, June 11, 1987
2. Name of congressman giving this address
   Mr. Fascell

Using the 1985 ASI, find a report giving the results of police response to crimes in San Diego and answer the following:

1. Title of the report
   Calling the police: citizen reporting of serious crime
2. Documents classification number for that report
   J28.2:C 13/2

Using the 1985 *Index*,. find an article on how spanking a child can be a form of child abuse and answer the following:

1. Author and title of article
   Ralph S. Welsh. Spanking: a grand old American tradition
2. Title of periodical containing the article
   Children today
3. Volume number, issue number, and page reference for that article
   14/1/25–29
4. Documents class number for that periodical
   HE23.1209:

John M. Ross is head of the Government Publications Section of the California State University Library in Los Angeles. He is also the author of *Foreign Trade Publications in United States Documents* (Council of Planning Librarians, 1987).